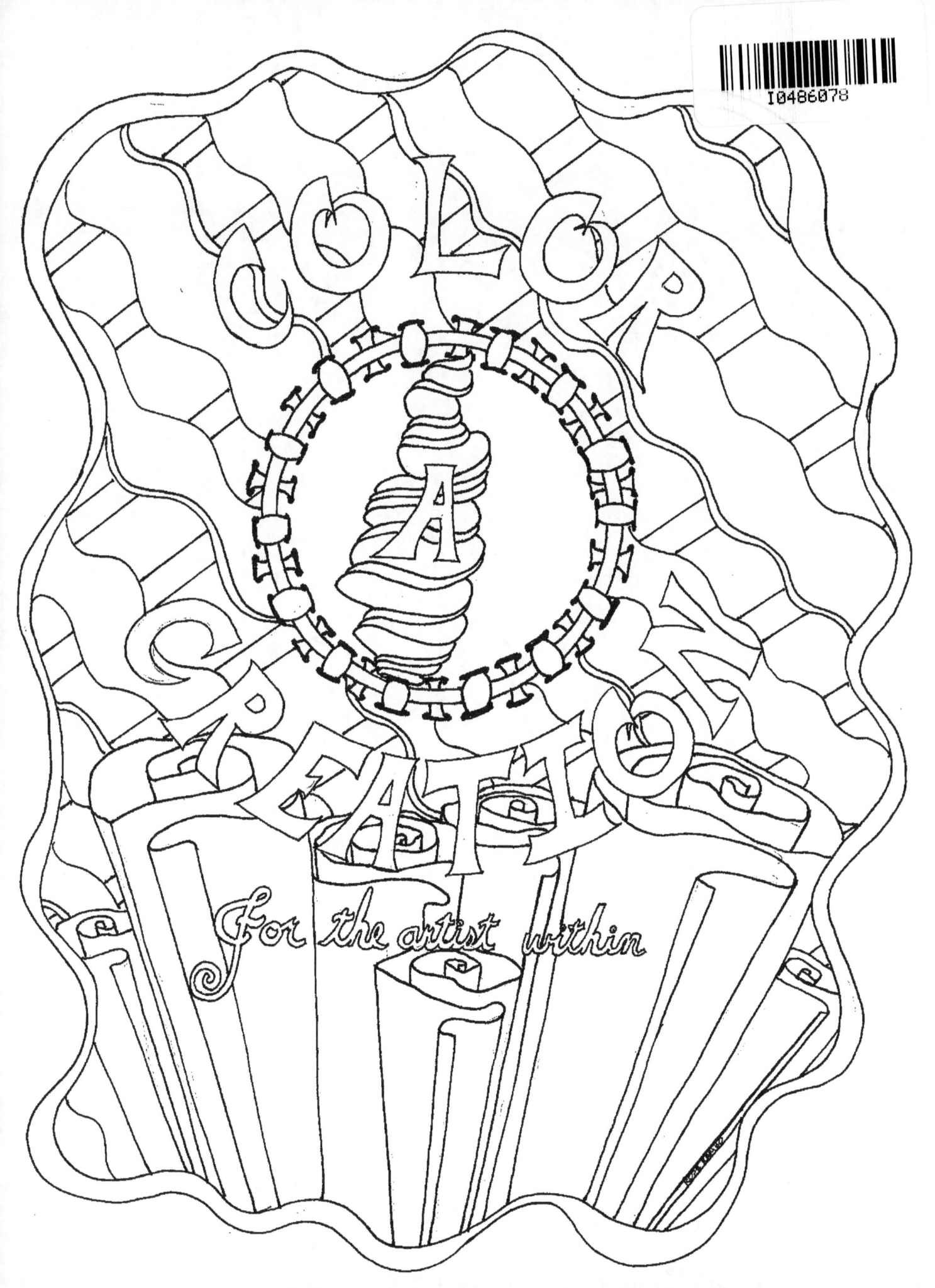

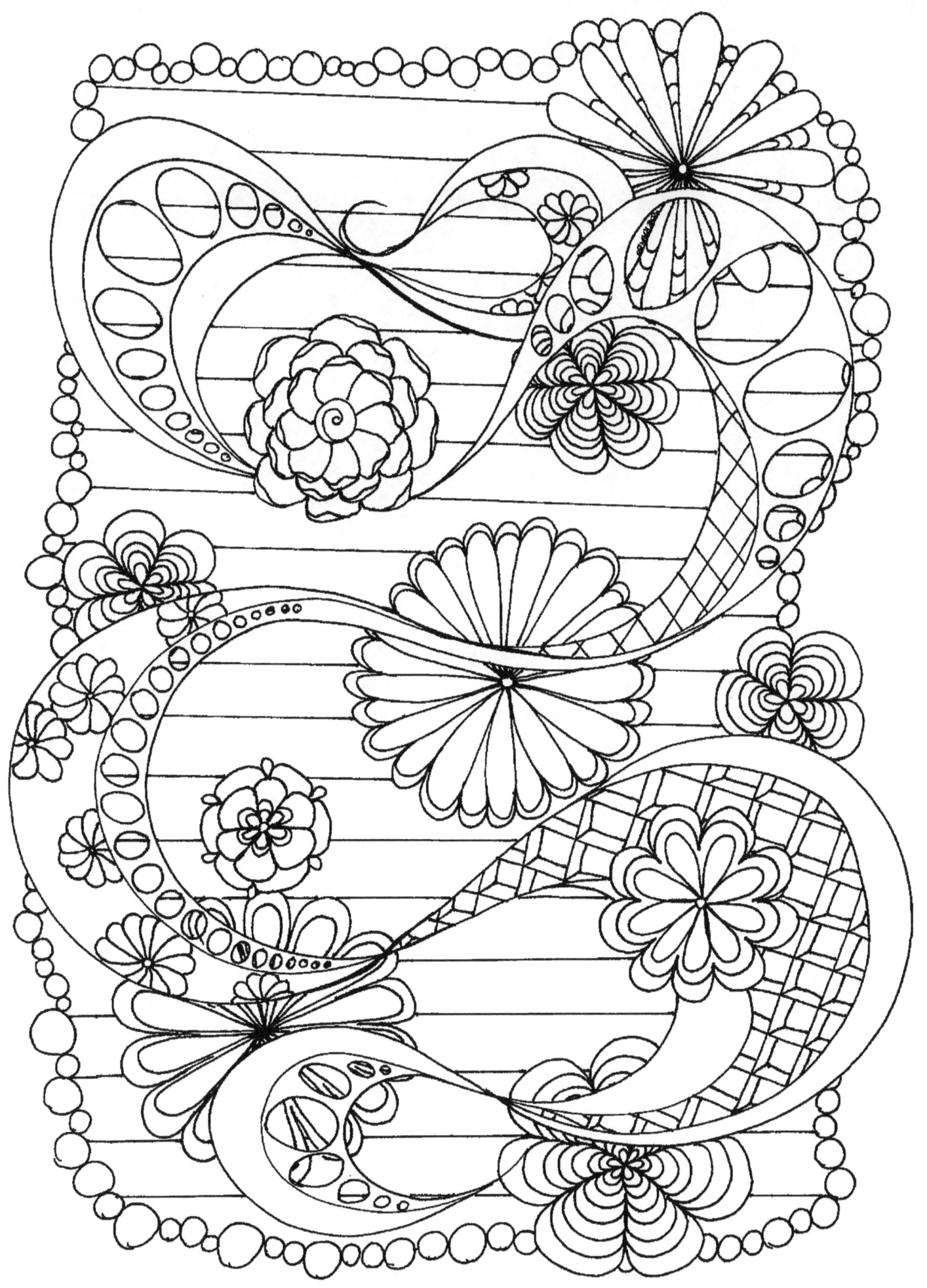

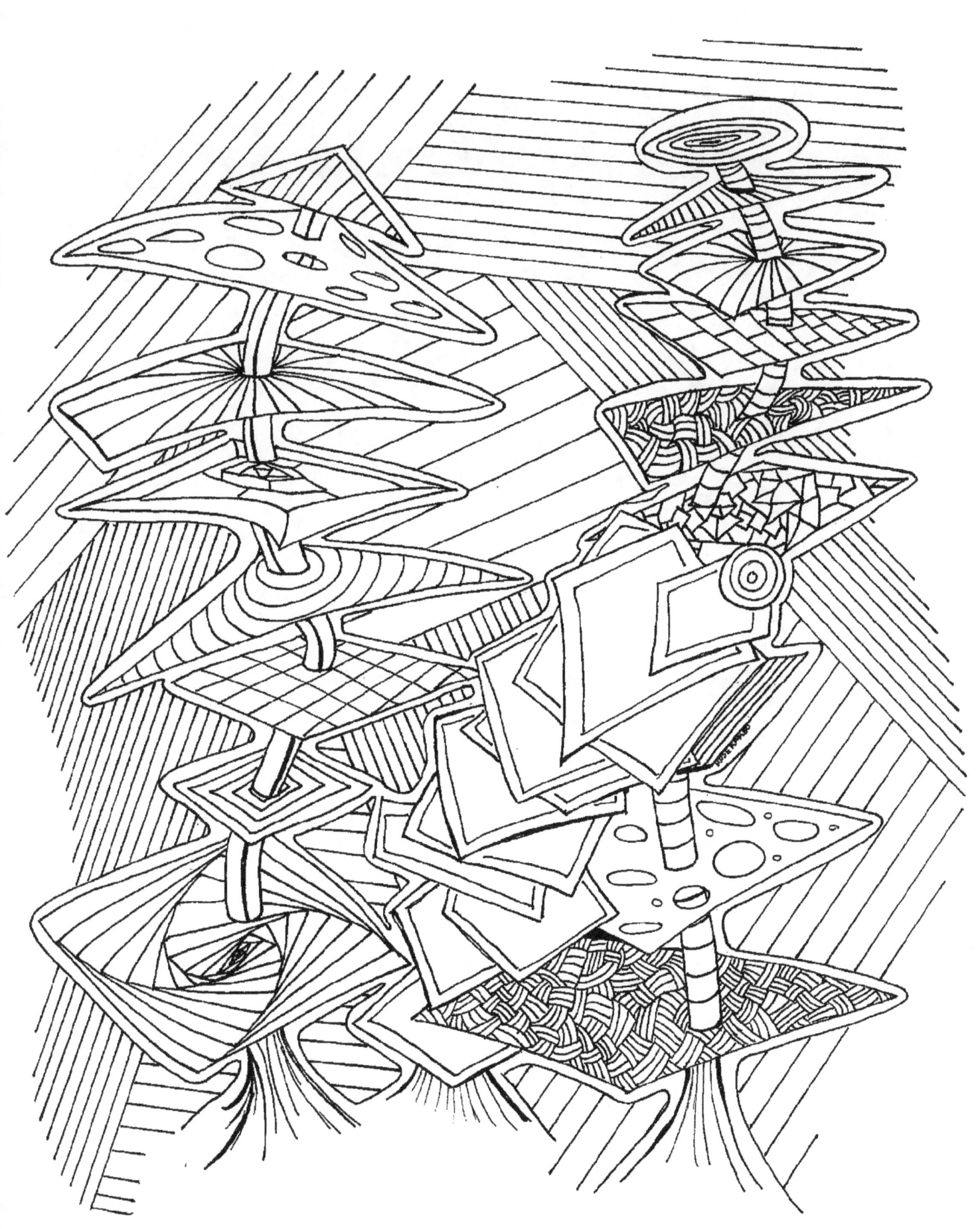

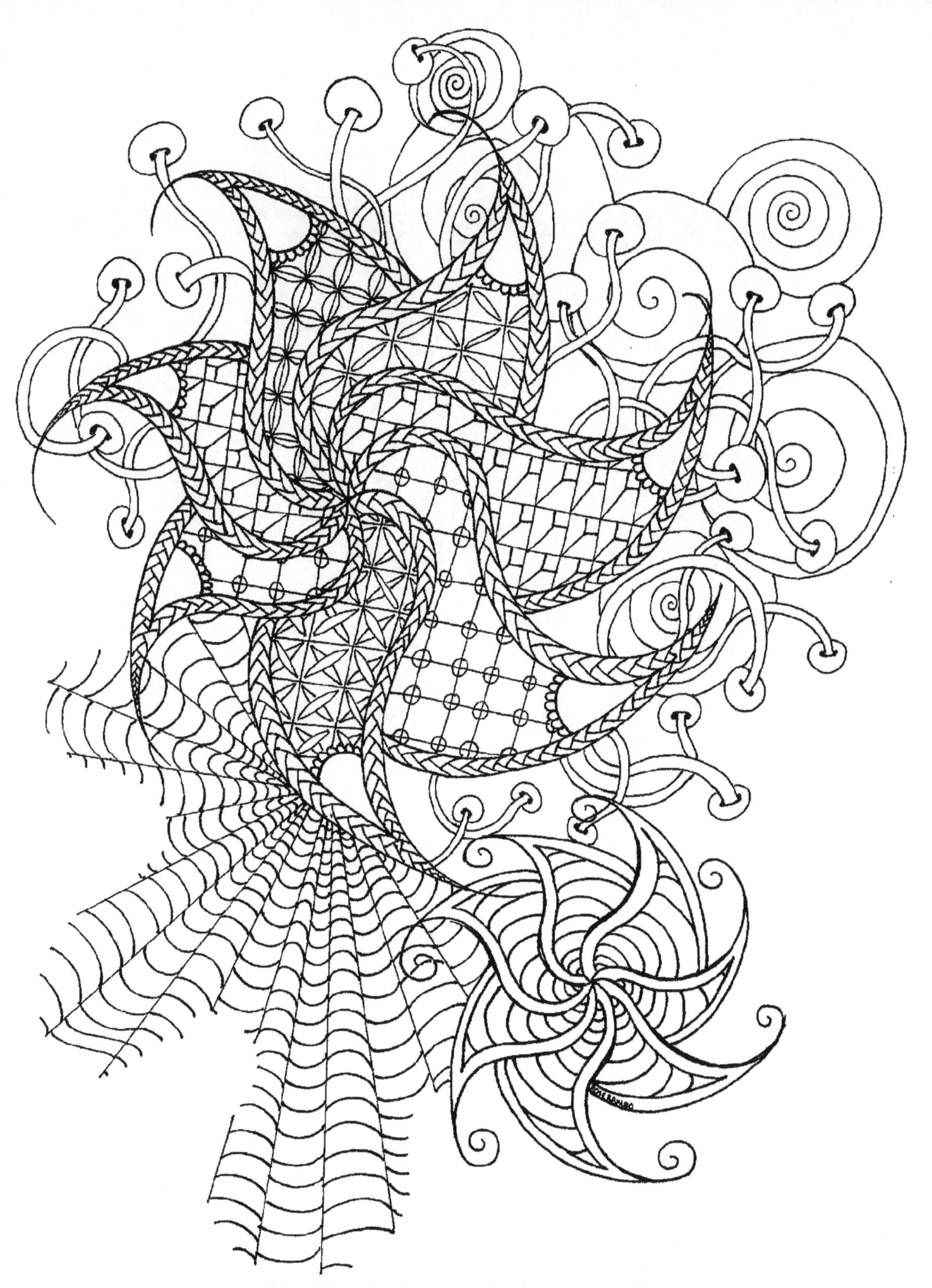

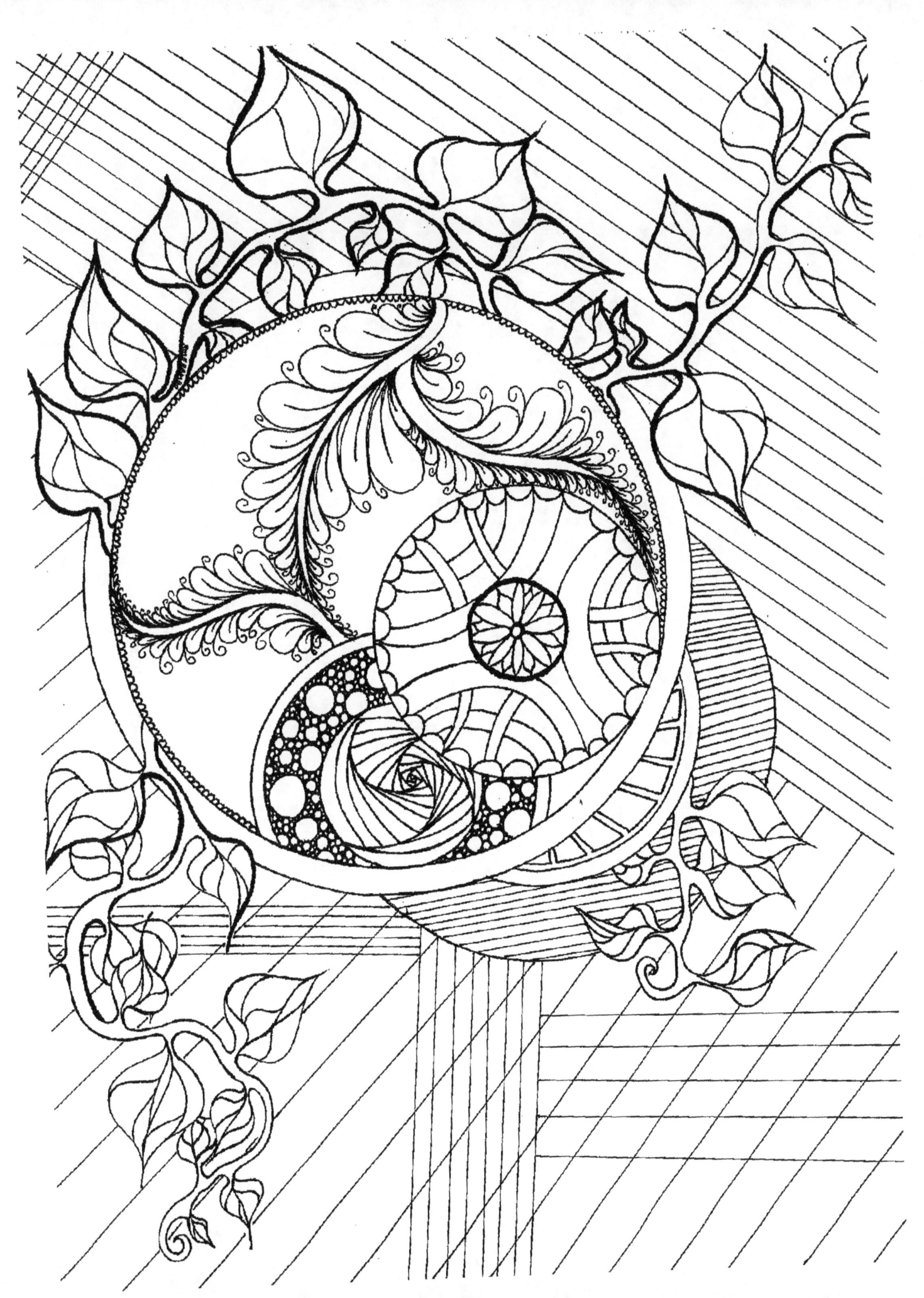

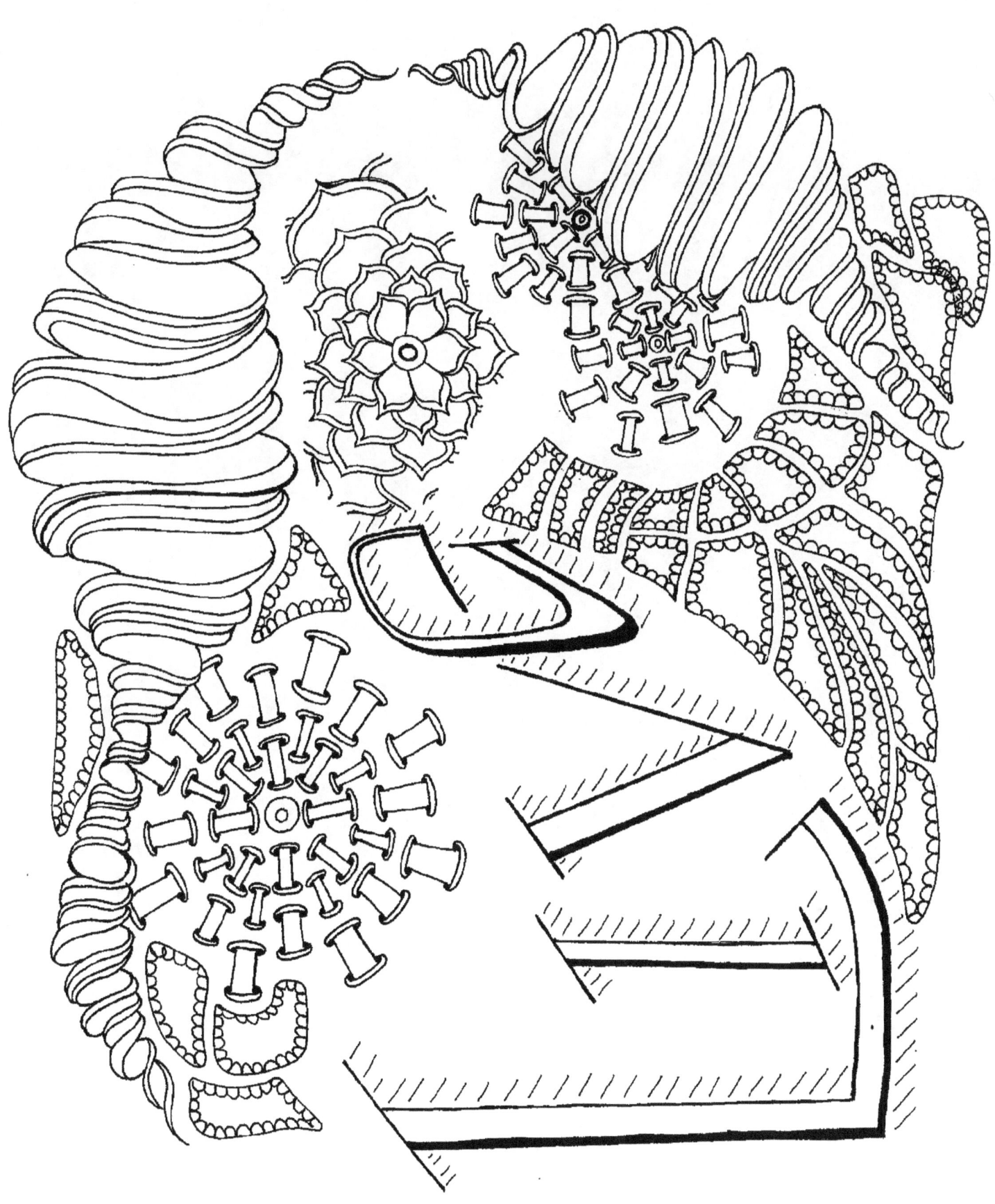

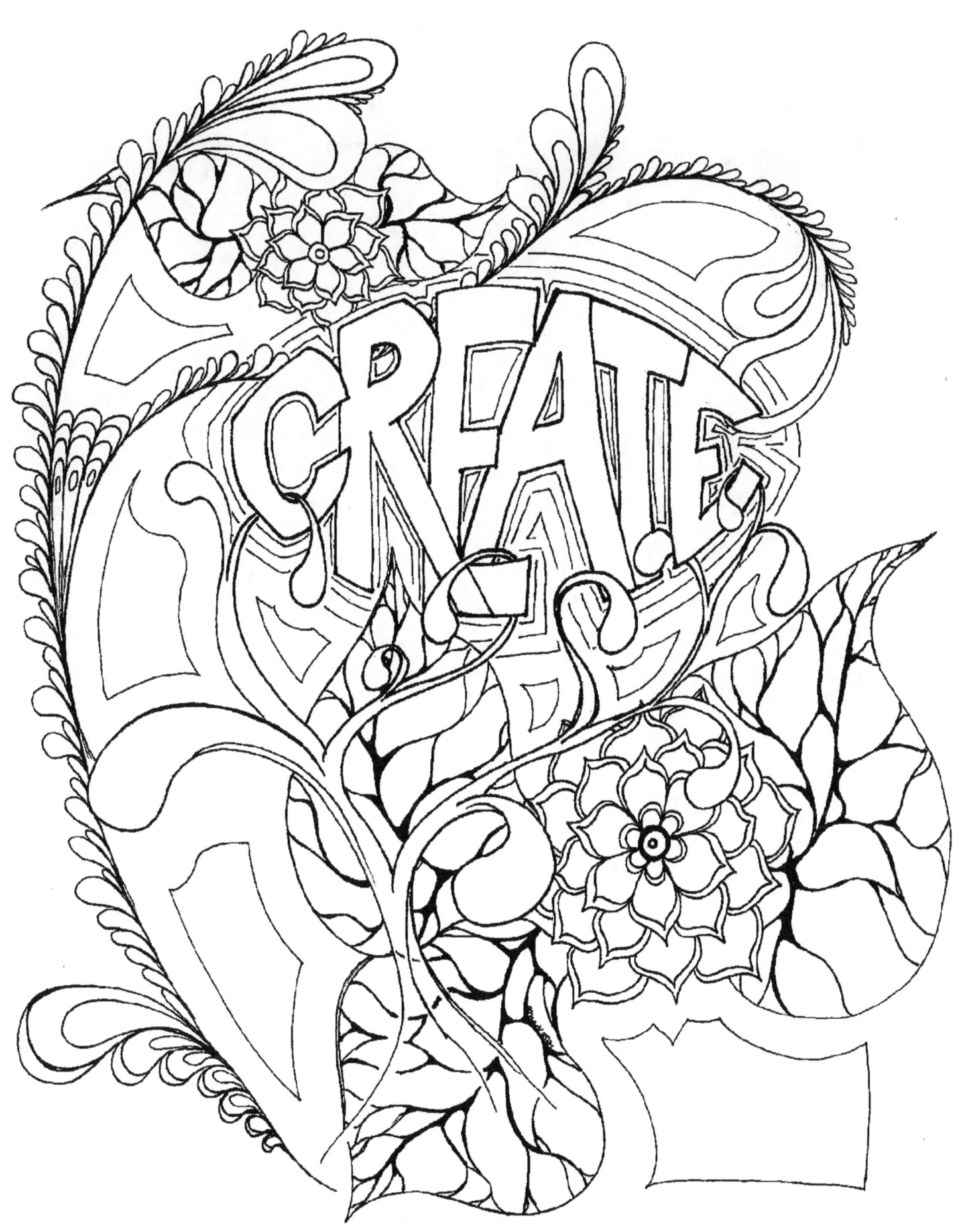

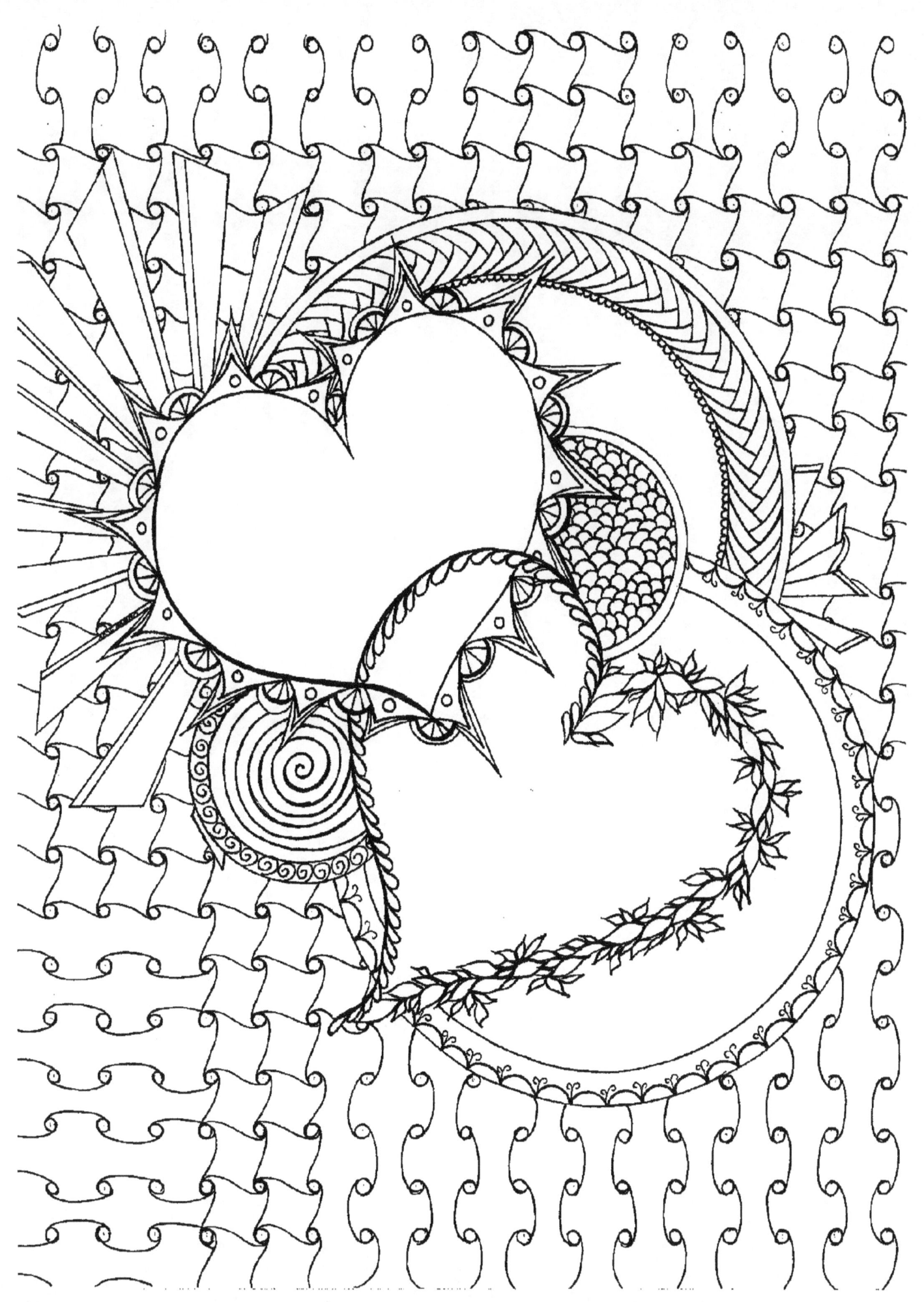

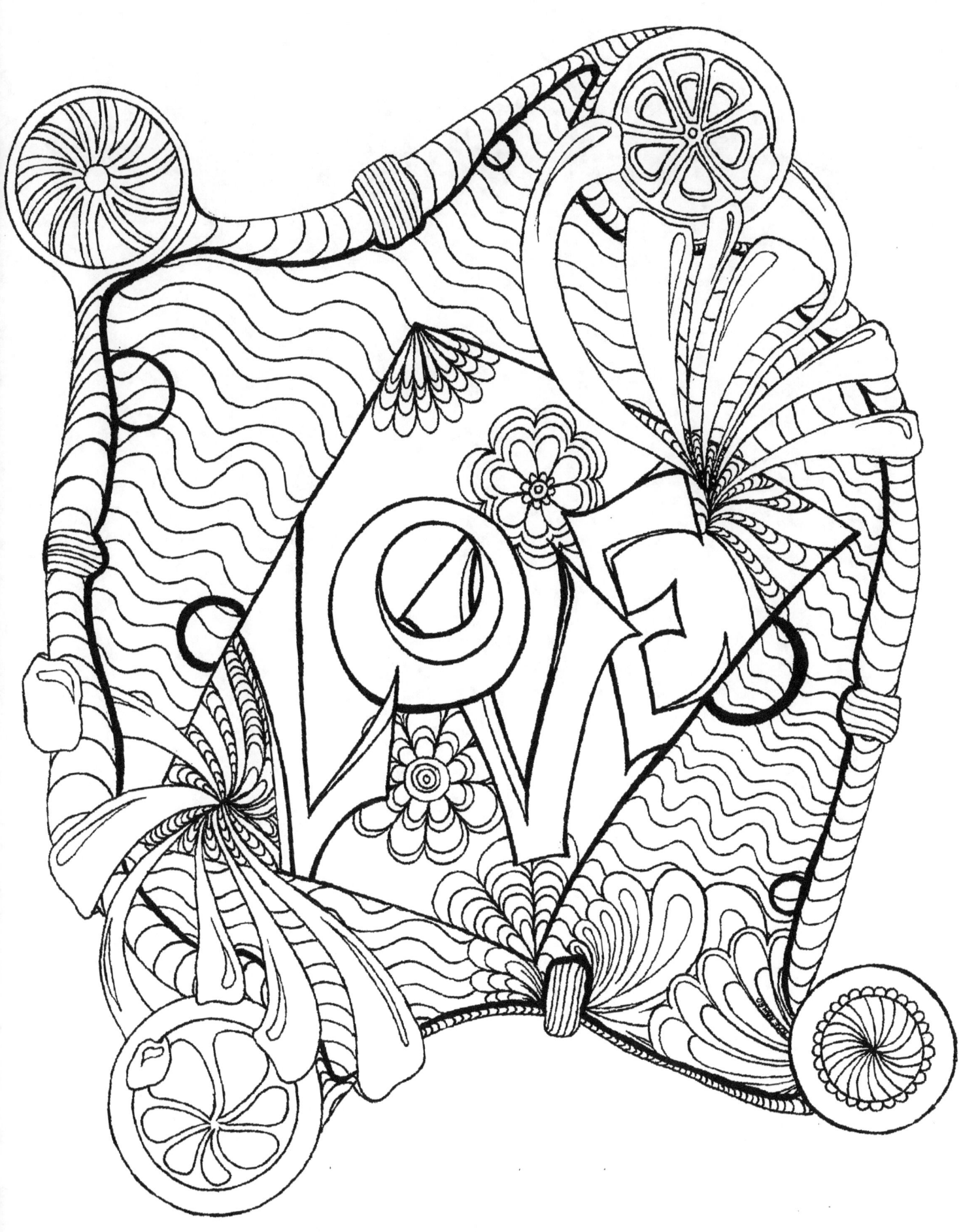

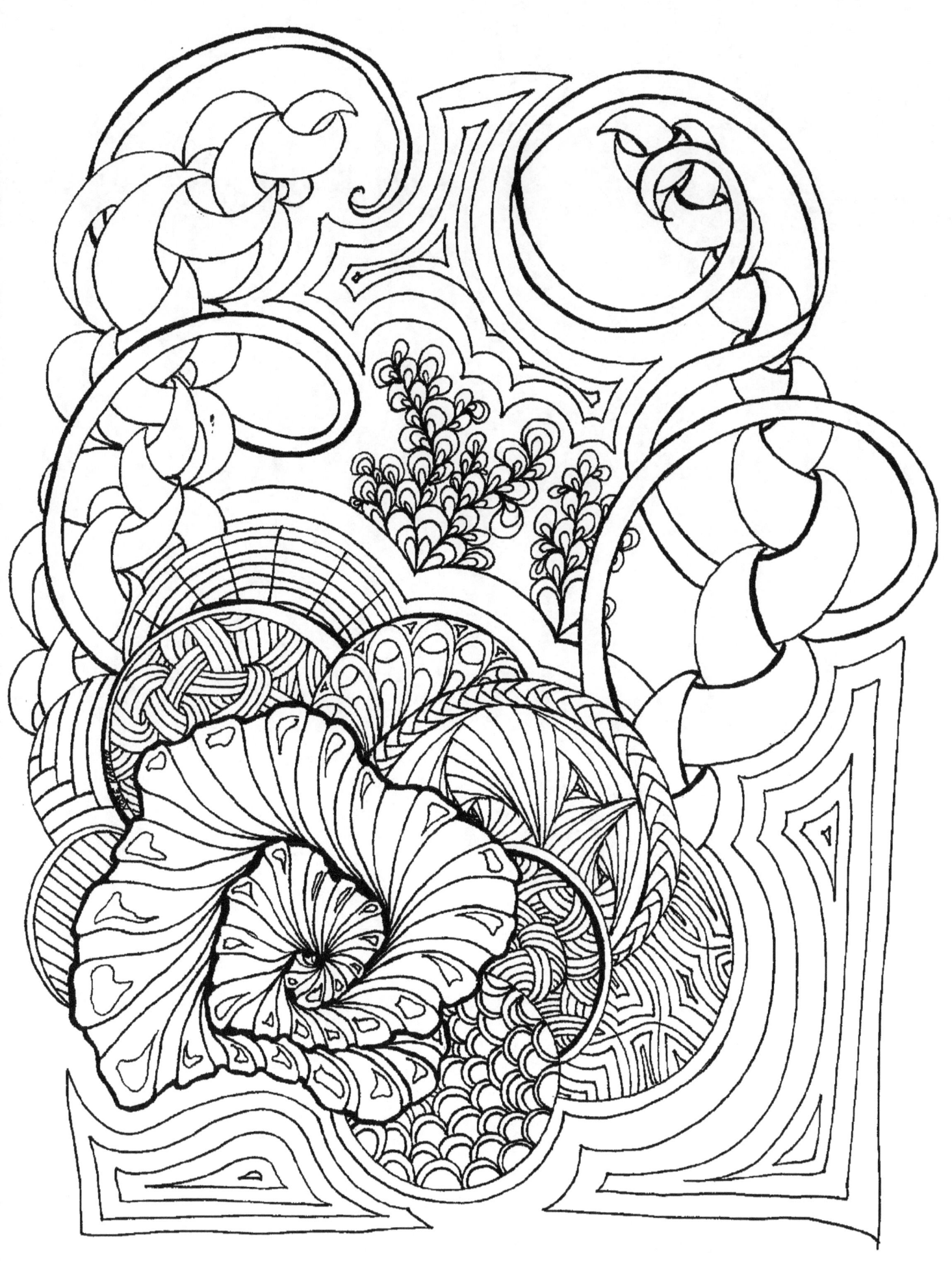

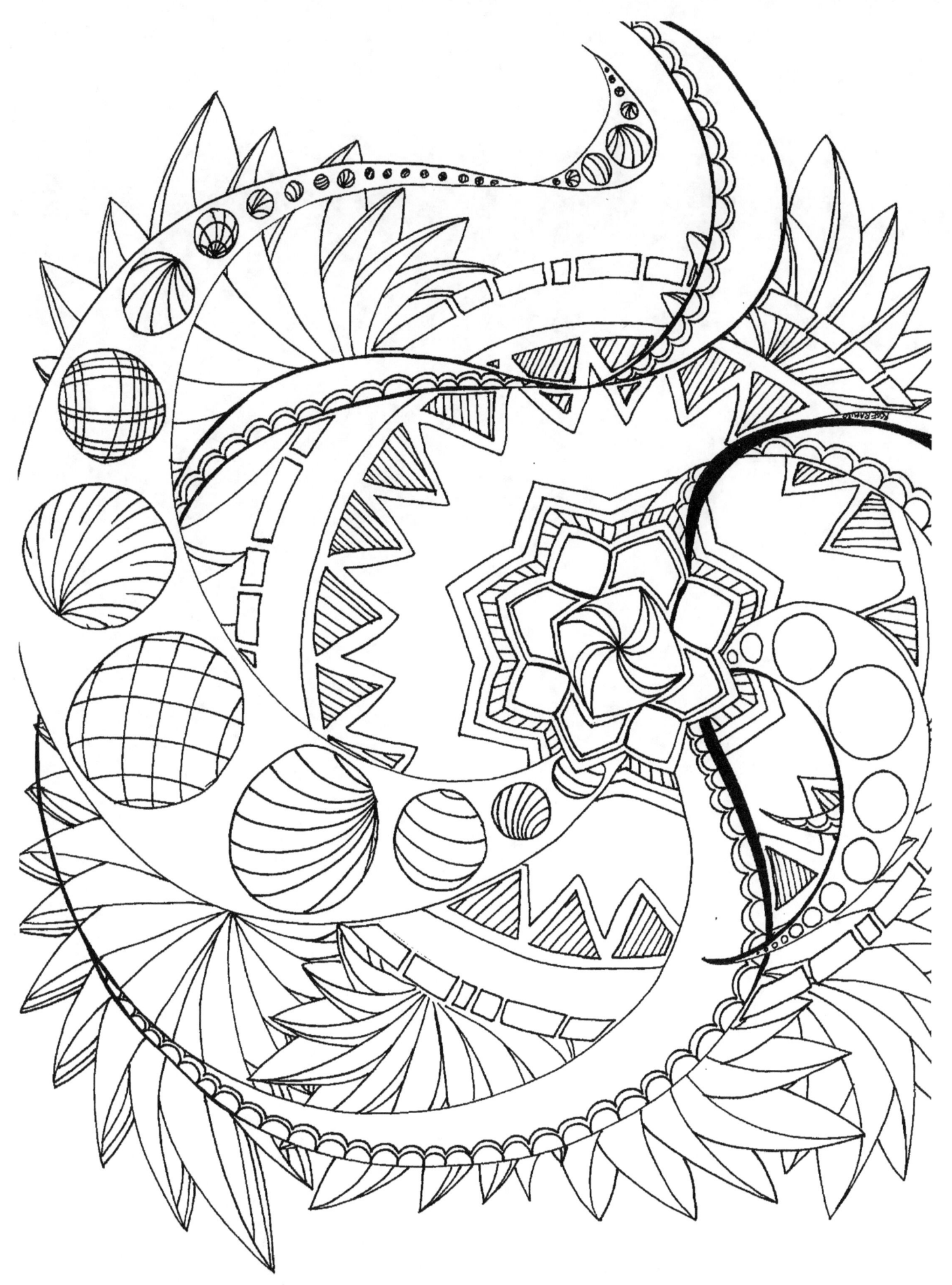

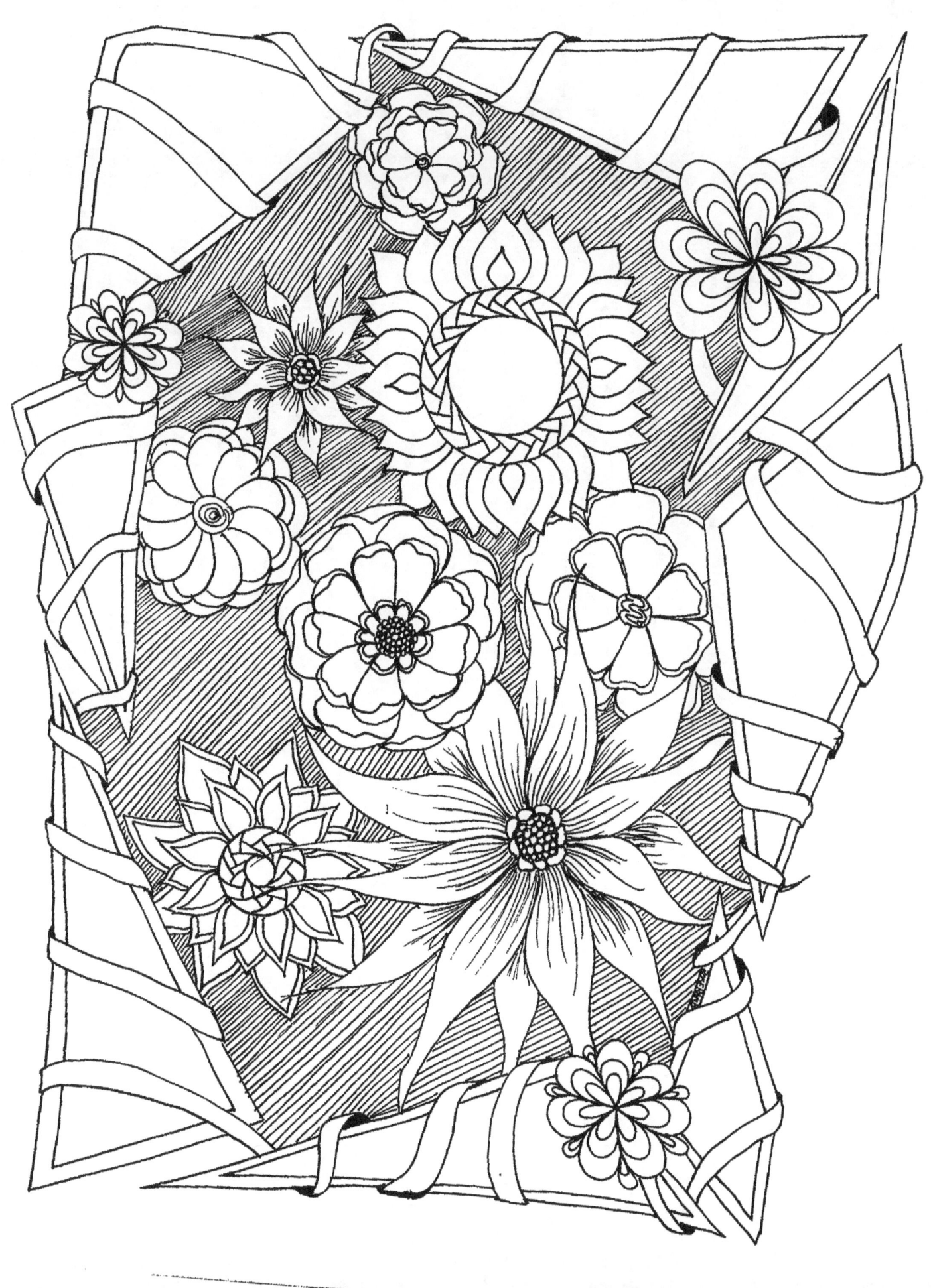

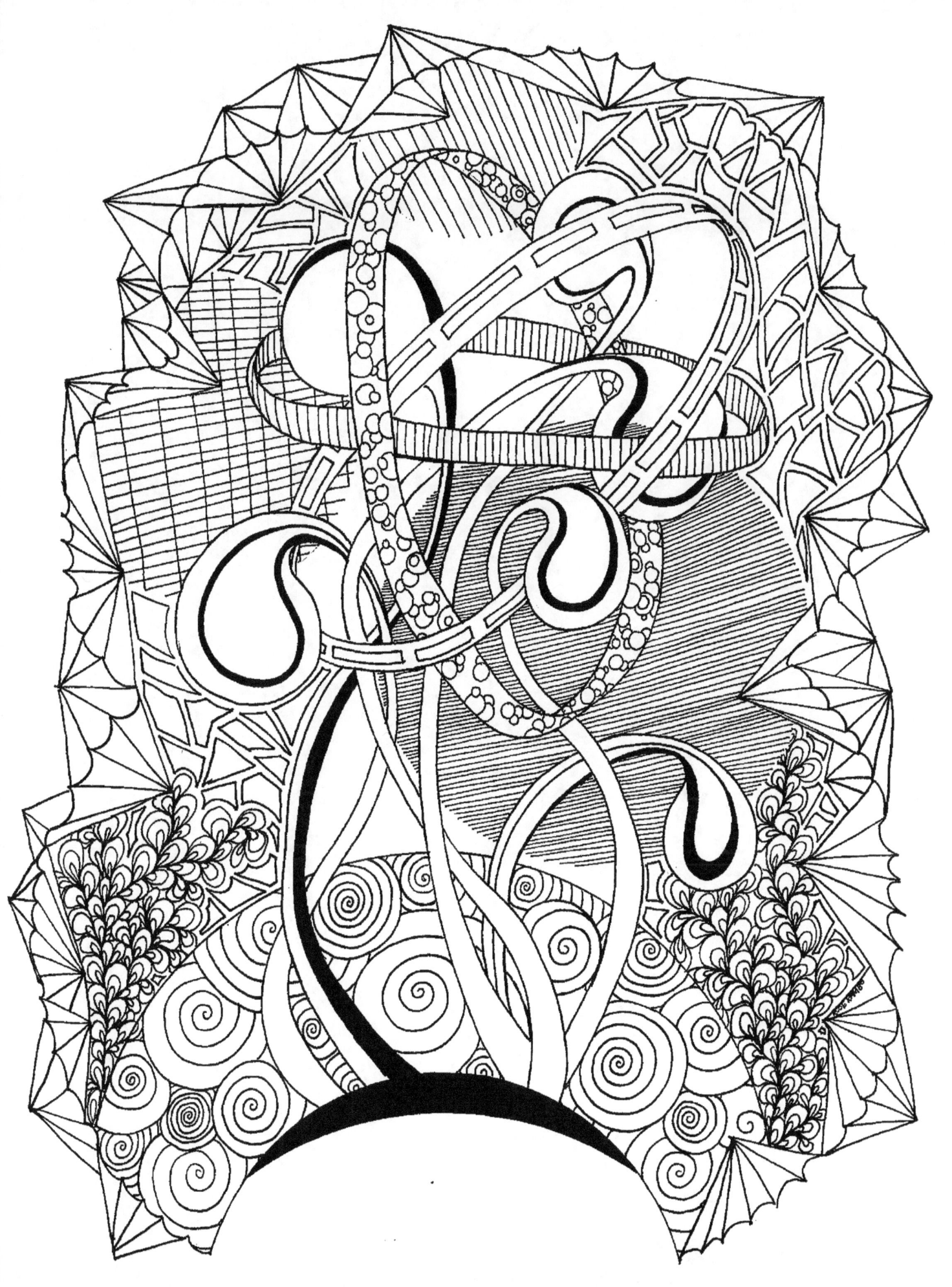

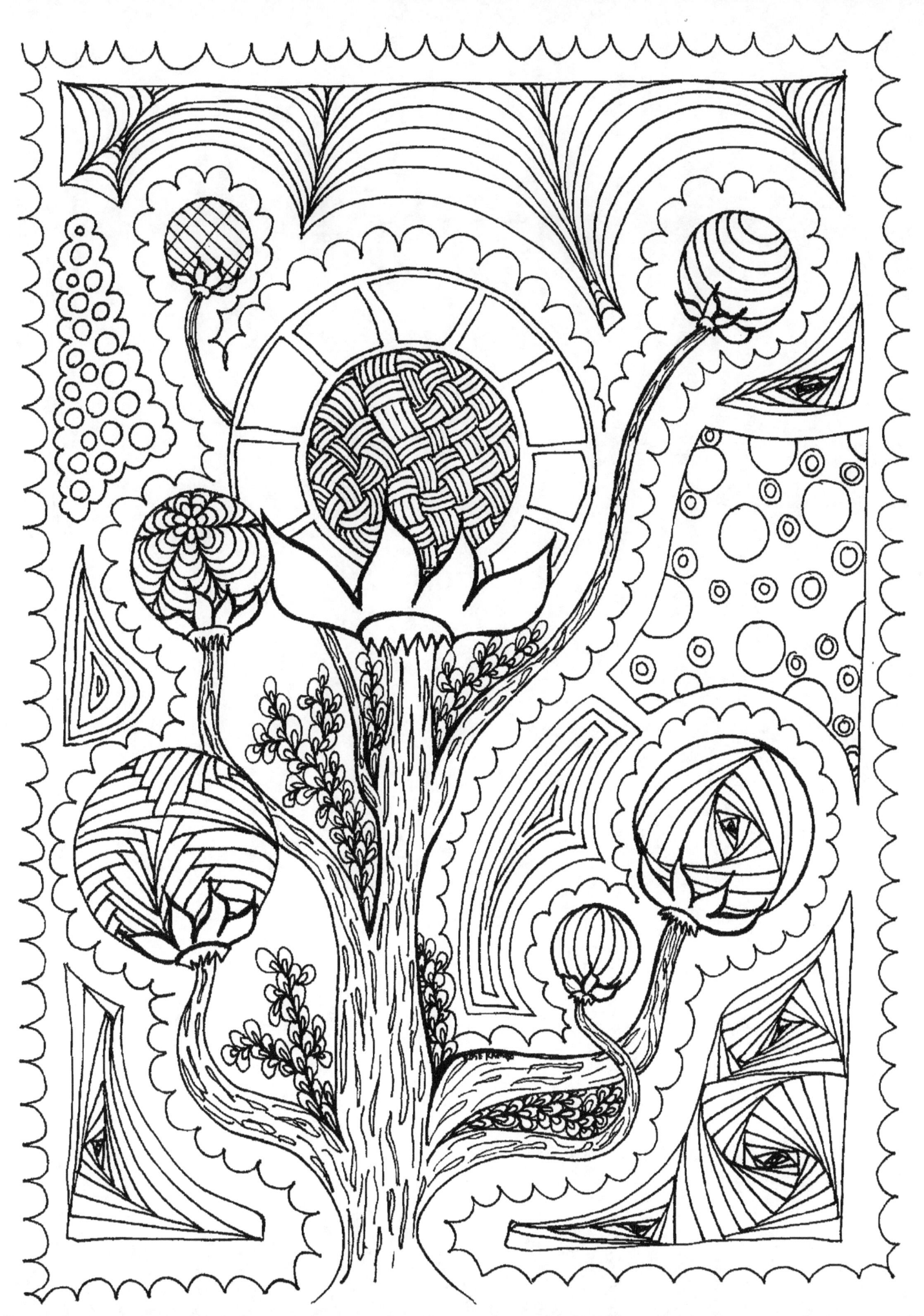

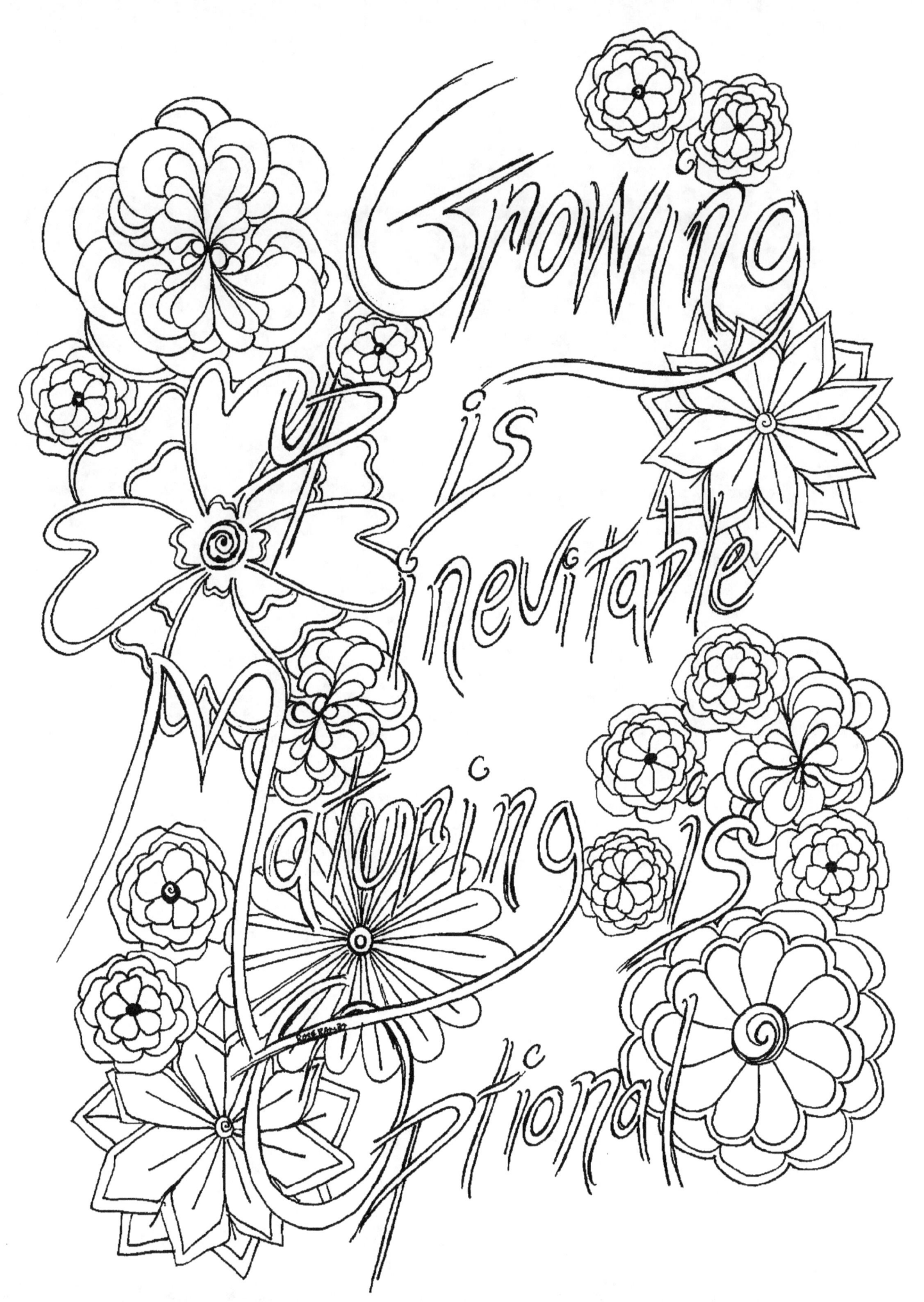

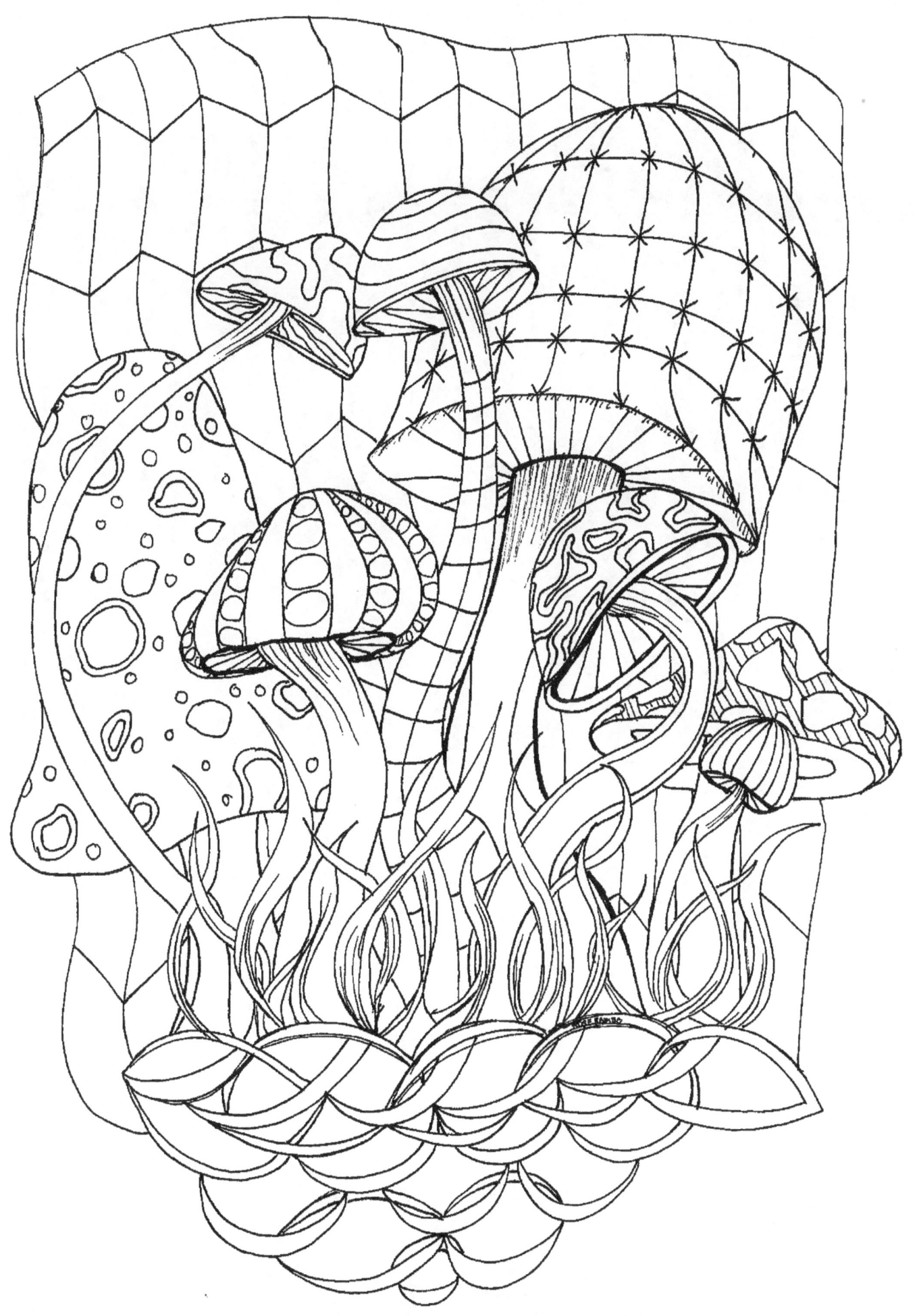

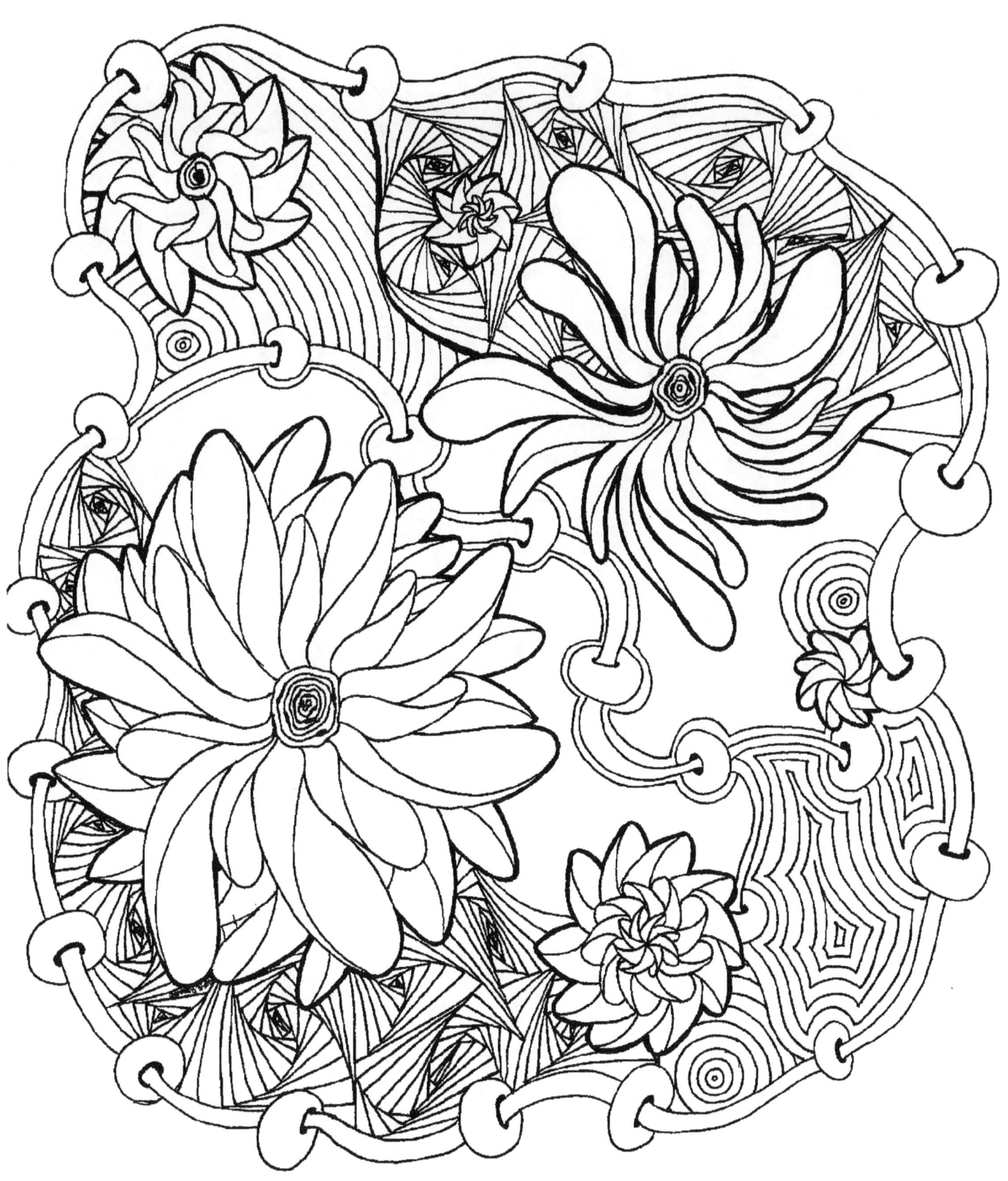

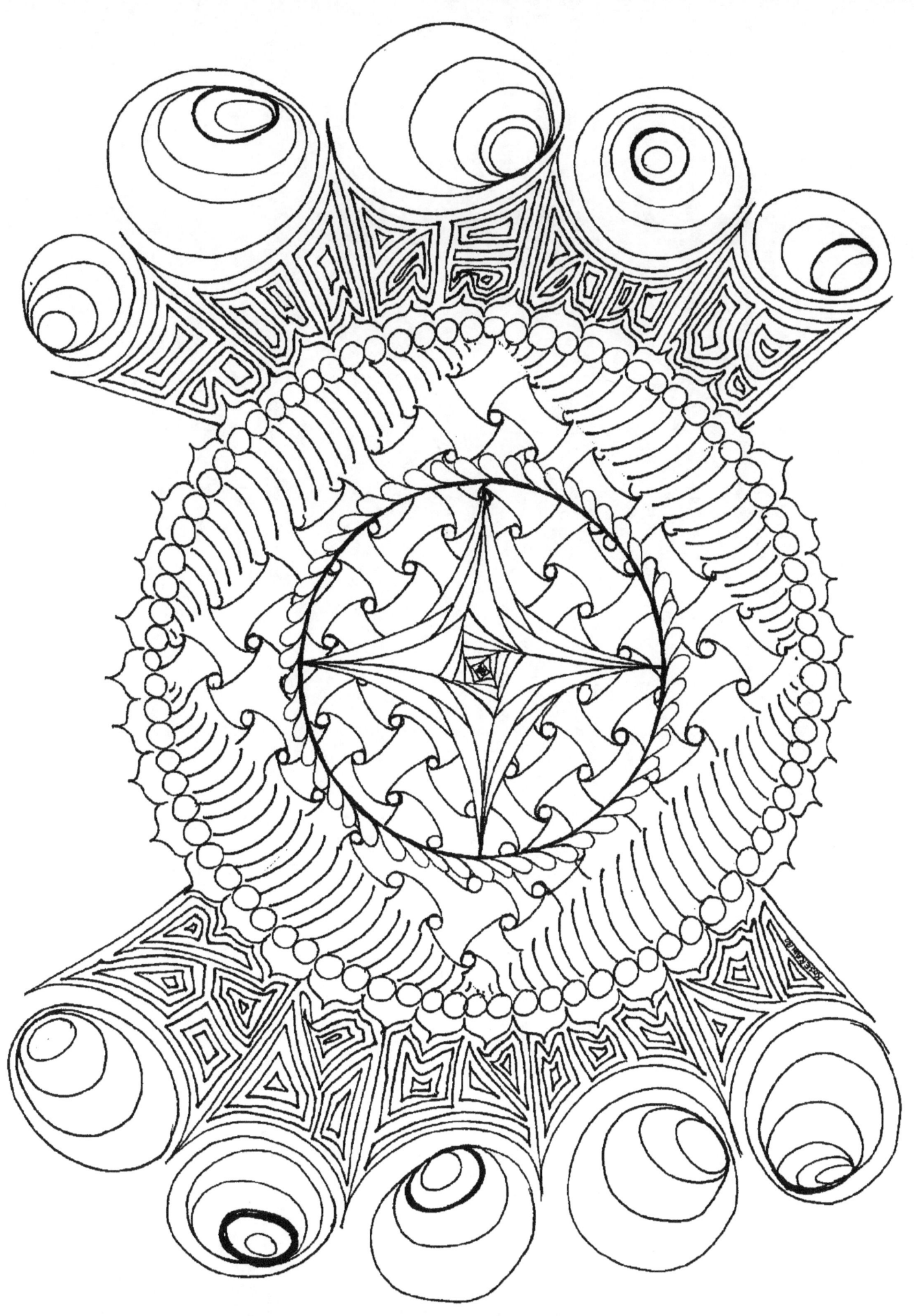

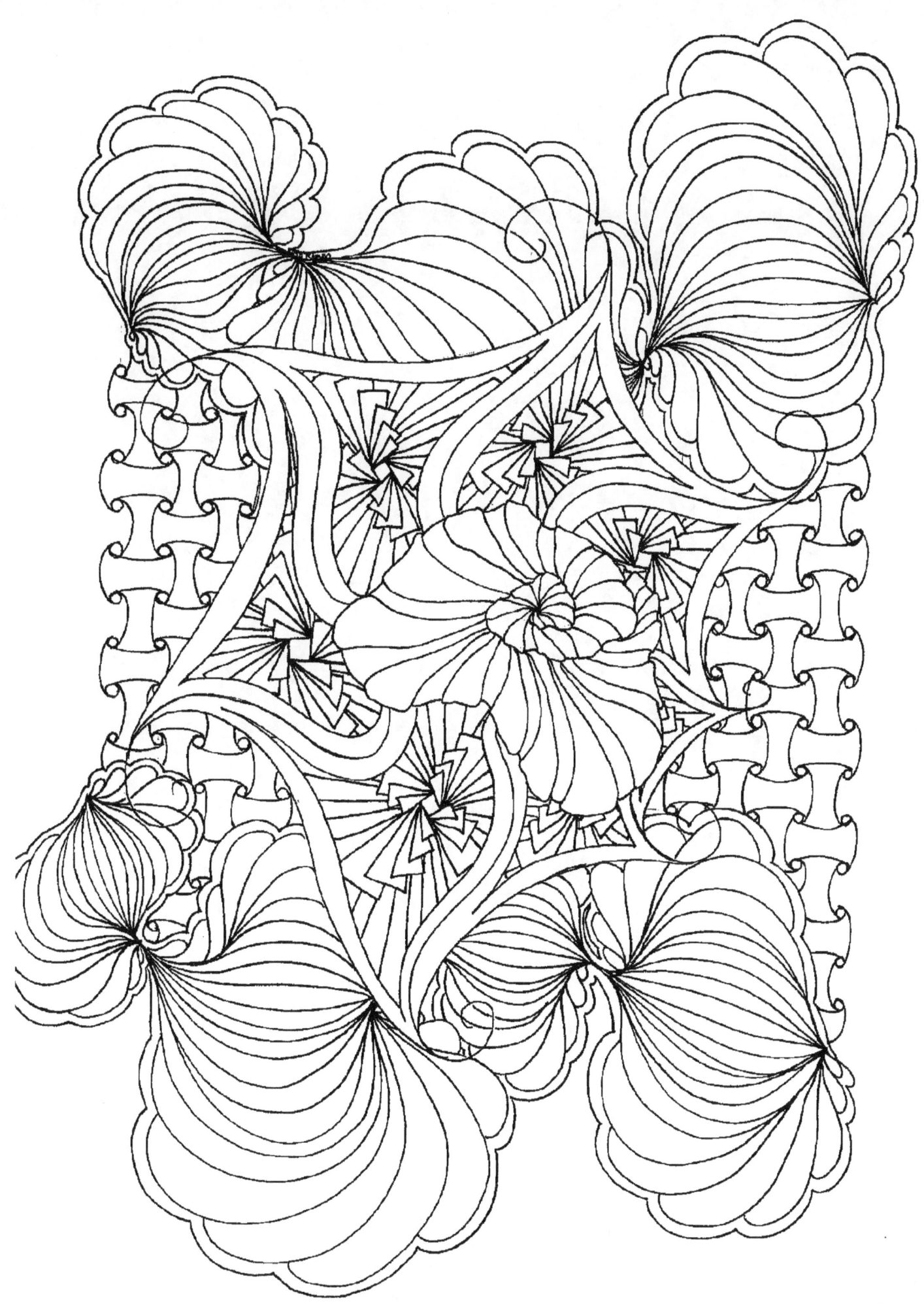

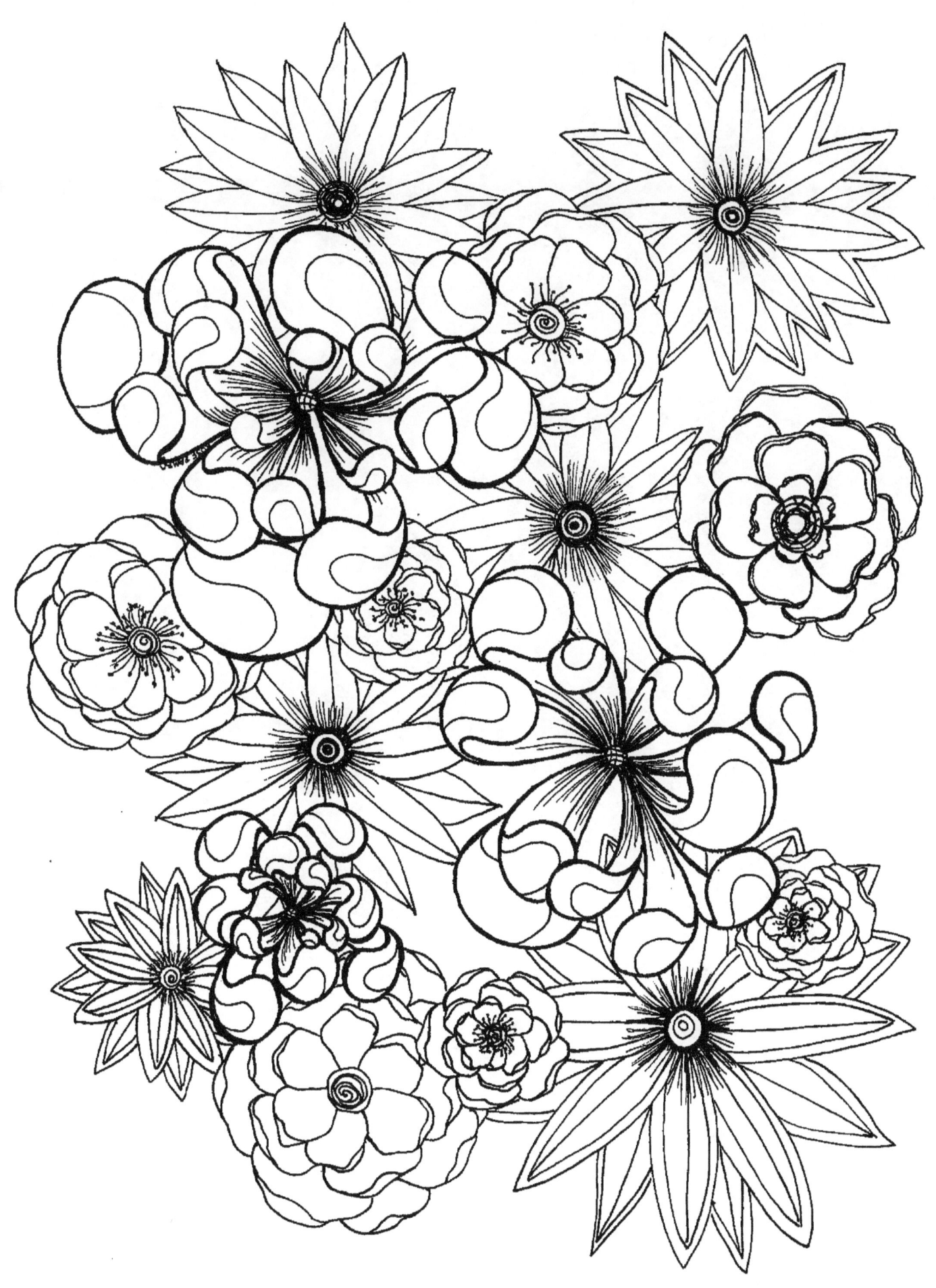

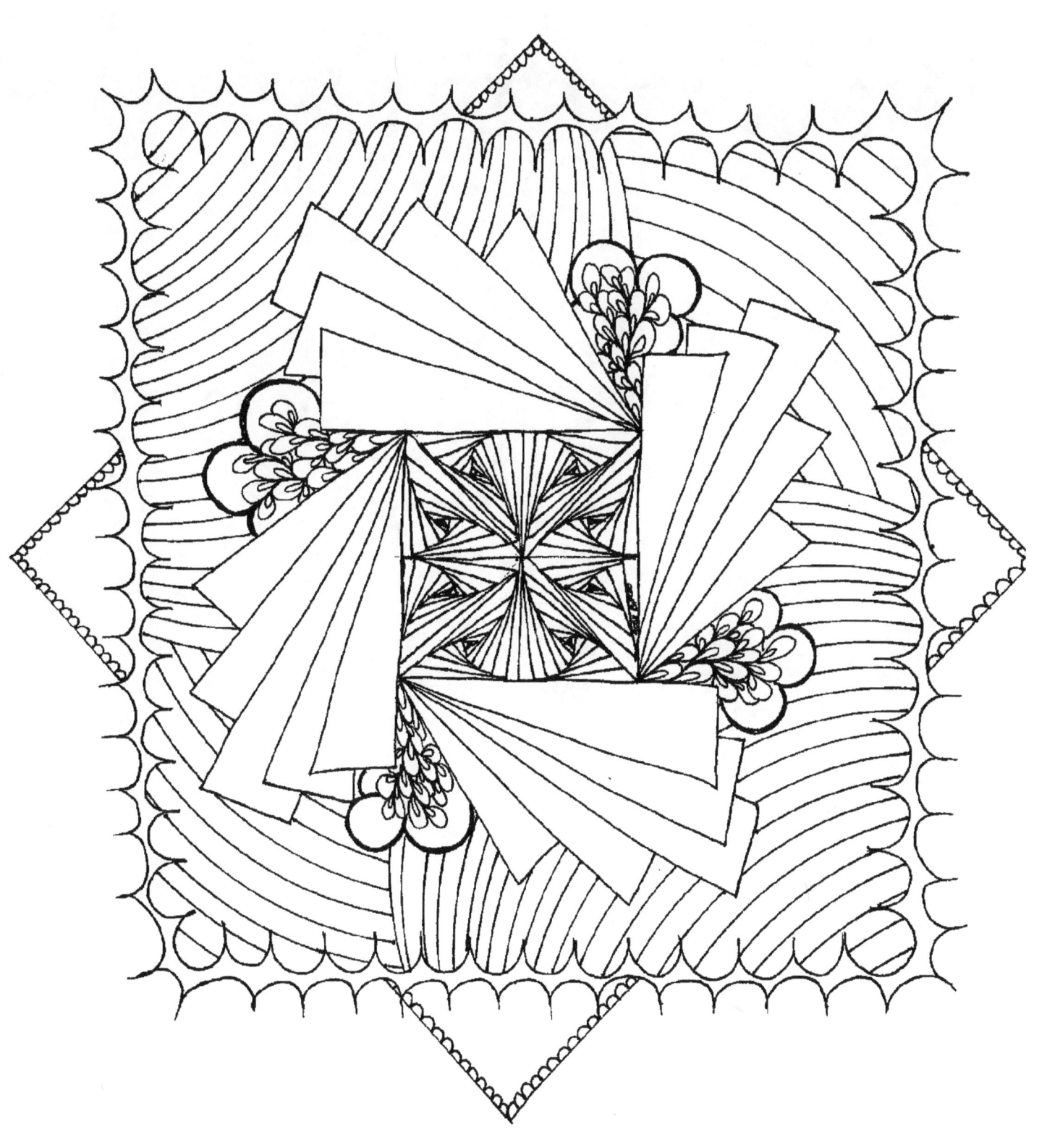

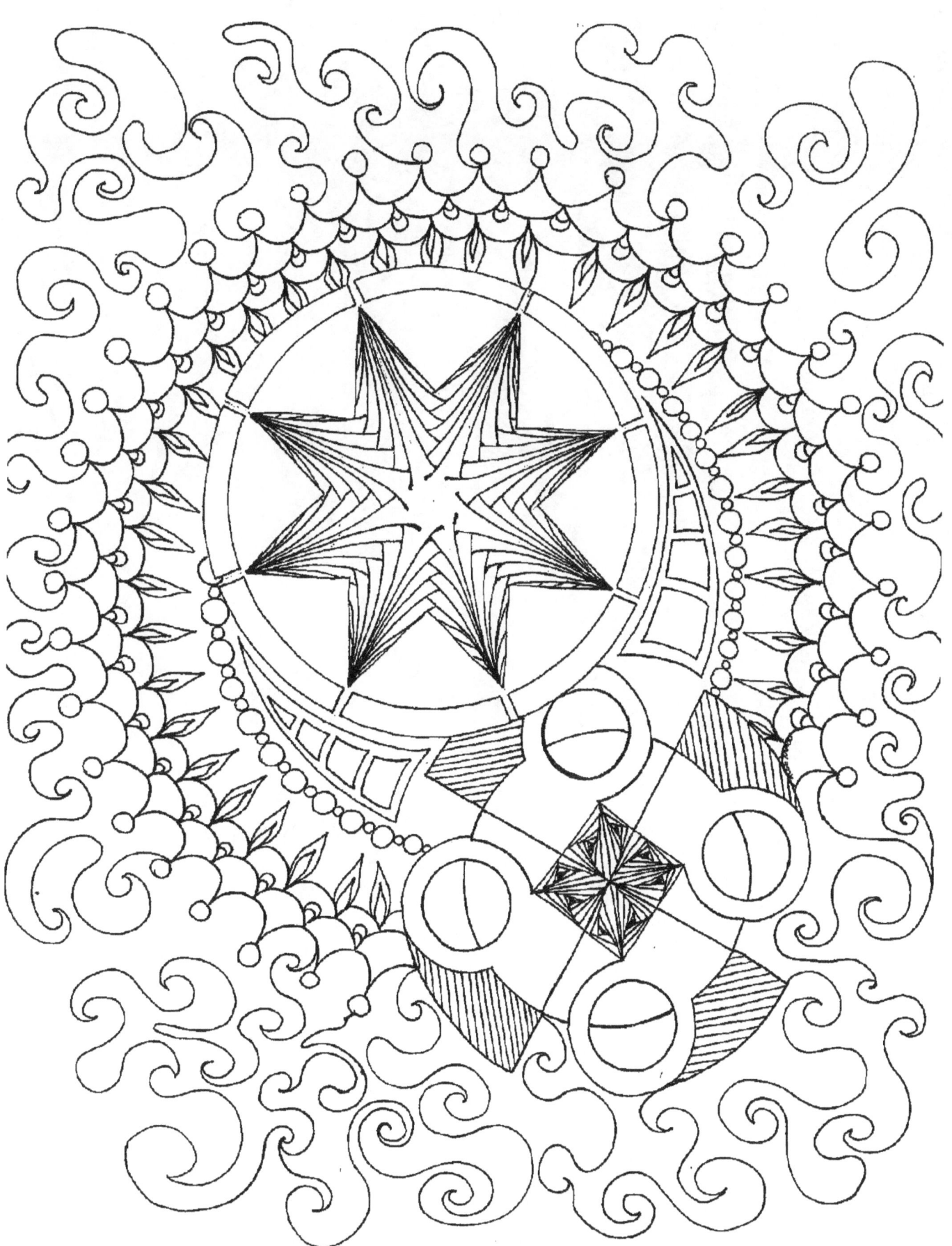

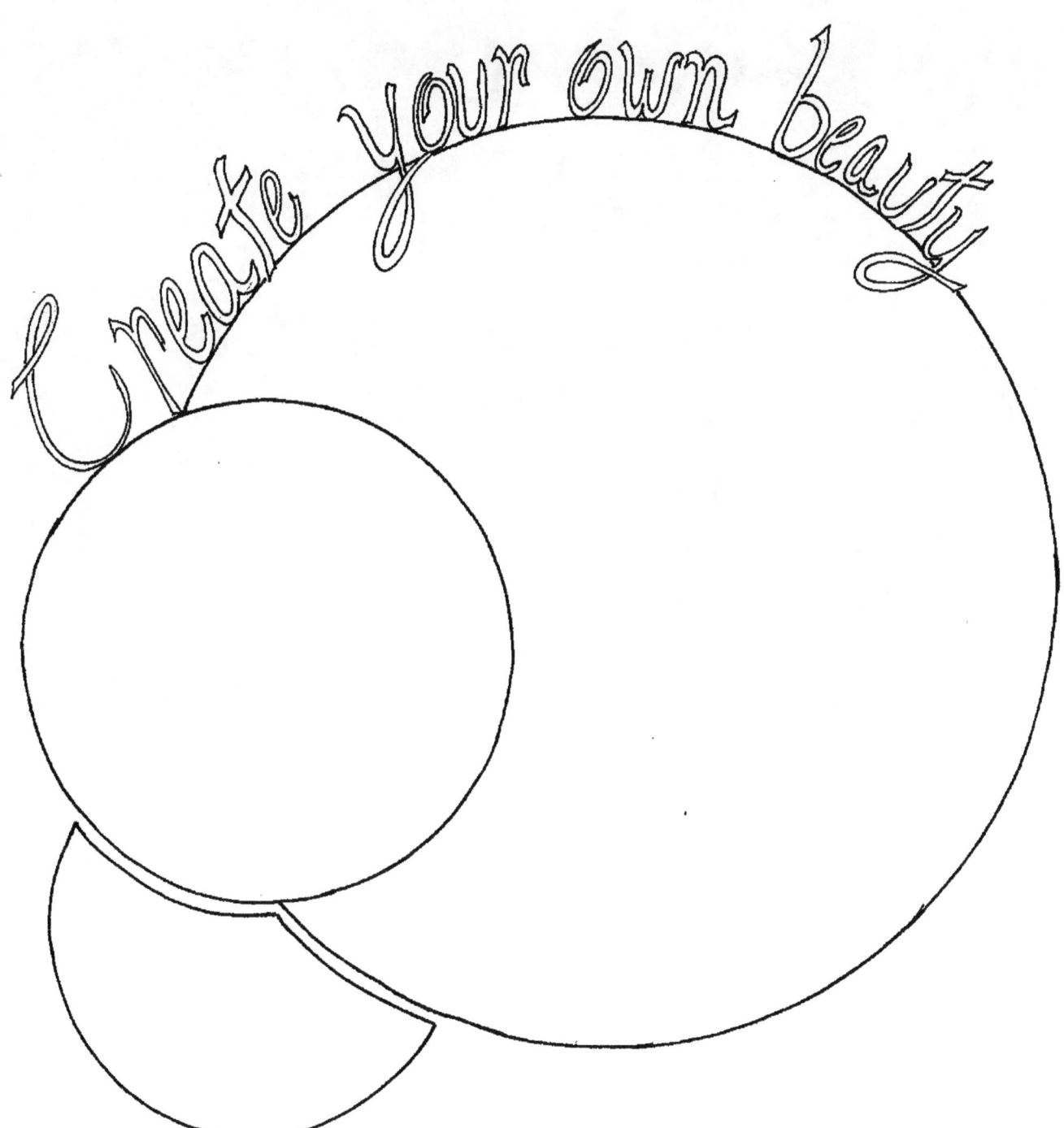

Create your own beauty

About the artist.

Rose Rambo is a visionary artist worth following. She has the unique ability to translate the creative inspiration of innocence to paper and canvas. Mrs. Rambo brings joy and inspiration to adults through the creative play of rediscovering the joy of color.

Mrs. Rambo was home schooled and began her studies at Tarrant County College at the age of sixteen. She continued her studies in art at Abilene Christian University. She works in acrylics, watercolor, pen and ink. Rose's attention to detail has created a demand for commissioned portrait work. Her photographic memory provides an endless library of ideas and inspiration.

Rose is a native Texan, born in San Antonio and raised in Fort Worth. She lives with her husband and two cats. Rose looks forward to new opportunities to bring joy, inspiration, and beauty to the world around her.

Rose Rambo's art: where passion comes to life.

www.facebook.com/vitruvianart

RoseRamboArt@gmail.com